THE GREAT DEPRESSION

Robin Johnson

CRABTREE
Publishing Company
www.crabtreebooks.com

Crabtree Publishing Company
www.crabtreebooks.com

Author: Robin Johnson
Publishing plan research and development: Reagan Miller
Editors: Rachel Minay, Kathy Middleton
Proofreader: Adrianna Morganelli
Photo researchers: Robin Johnson, Rachel Minay
Book design: Tim Mayer
Cover design: Ken Wright
Production coordinator and prepress tecnician: Ken Wright
Print coordinator: Margaret Amy Salter

Produced for Crabtree Publishing Company by White-Thomson Publishing

Photographs:
Corbis: pp. 32–33; Bettmann: pp. 11, 22–23, 42–43; Blue Lantern Studio: pp8–9; Blue Lantern Studio/Laughing E/Blue Lantern Studio: pp. 16–17; Elena Tiniakou/Demotix: p. 44; Hulton-Deutsch Collection: pp. 14–15; Minnesota Historical Society: pp. 18–19; Getty: AFP/Getty Images: p. 45; Hulton Collection: pp. 40–41; Library of Congress: pp. 1, 3, 12–13, 26, 28–29, 33; Shutterstock: Andrew Zarivny: p. 37; SeanPavonePhoto: p. 10; SuperStock: Album/Album: p. 35; Topfoto: The Granger Collection: pp. 4, 6–7, 27, 30–31, 34; White–Thomson Publishing/Stefan Chabluk: p. 25; Wikimedia: pp. 5, 13, 20–21, 24, 36, 38; Wikimedia Commons: U.S. National Archives and Records Administration: front cover; © Zim235/Dreamstime.com: back cover

Library and Archives Canada Cataloguing in Publication

Johnson, Robin (Robin R.), author
    The Great Depression / Robin Johnson.

(Crabtree chrome)
Includes index.
Issued in print and electronic formats.
ISBN 978-0-7787-1173-5 (bound).--ISBN 978-0-7787-1186-5 (pbk.).--
ISBN 978-1-4271-8934-9 (pdf).--ISBN 978-1-4271-8926-4 (html)

    1. Depressions--1929--Juvenile literature. I. Title.
II. Series: Crabtree chrome

E806.J64 2013   j973.917   C2013-906226-2
                              C2013-906227-0

Library of Congress Cataloging-in-Publication Data

Johnson, Robin (Robin R.)
    The Great Depression / Robin Johnson.
      pages cm. -- (Crabtree chrome)
    Includes index.
    ISBN 978-0-7787-1173-5 (reinforced library binding : alk. paper) -- ISBN 978-0-7787-1186-5 (pbk. : alk. paper) -- ISBN 978-1-4271-8934-9 (electronic pdf) -- ISBN 978-1-4271-8926-4 (electronic html)
    1. United States--History--1933-1945--Juvenile literature.
2. United States--History--1919-1933--Juvenile literature.
3. Depressions--1929--United States--Juvenile literature. 4. New Deal, 1933-1939--Juvenile literature. 5. United States--Economic conditions--1918-1945--Juvenile literature. I. Title.

E806.J65 2014
973.916--dc23

                          2013036063

Crabtree Publishing Company
www.crabtreebooks.com   1-800-387-7650

Printed in Canada/012014/BF20131120

Published in Canada
Crabtree Publishing
616 Welland Ave.
St. Catharines, ON
L2M 5V6

Published in the United States
Crabtree Publishing
PMB 59051
350 Fifth Avenue, 59th Floor
New York, New York 10118

Published in the United Kingdom
Crabtree Publishing
Maritime House
Basin Road North, Hove
BN41 1WR

Published in Australia
Crabtree Publishing
3 Charles Street
Coburg North
VIC 3058

Contents

The Roaring Twenties

We're in the Money

The 1920s began with a boom. After World War I, life was good for most people in North America and Europe. Businesses were booming, and there were plenty of jobs. Many people invested their money in the **stock market**. The value of stocks, or shares of companies, was always going up, so it seemed like an easy way to make more money. Everyone had high hopes and big plans for the future.

▼ *In the 1920s, the war had ended and the good times had begun!*

The Great Crash

On Tuesday, October 29, 1929, the world woke up to a great shock. In the United States, the price of many stocks dropped suddenly. When the price of a stock goes lower, people lose money. Panic spread. People rushed to sell their stocks before they became completely worthless. But many were too late. They lost all their savings. "Black Tuesday" was the beginning of a worldwide economic depression that would last a decade.

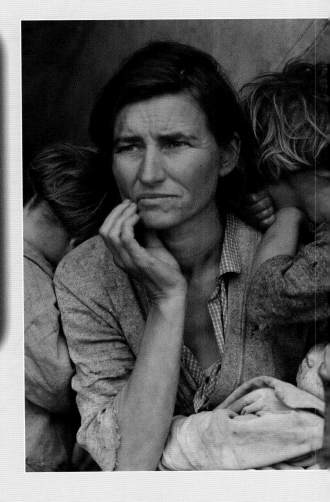

A depression is a period of time when businesses fail and many workers do not have jobs. The Great Depression began in 1929 in the United States but soon spread throughout the world. It did not end until World War II began in 1939.

▶ *Florence Owens Thompson became the face of the Great Depression. Like many mothers in the 1930s, she struggled to feed her family. They moved from place to place, finding work where they could.*

stock market: a place where stocks are bought and sold

Work and Play

The decade of the 1920s is nicknamed the "Roaring Twenties." The war was over and everyone was in a happy mood. New industries, such as automobile manufacturing, required a lot of workers. People worked hard and they had few worries.

◀ *People flocked to silent movies and jazz clubs in the 1920s.*

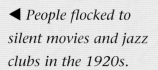

There was a "chicken in every pot. And a car in every backyard, to boot."

From a 1928 election poster for Herbert Hoover

Give Them Credit

People made money and spent it just as fast. They bought new cars, telephones, and radios. If shoppers could not afford the finer things in life, they used **credit** to buy them. People spent money they did not have—and bought more than they could afford.

credit: a way of buying goods but paying for them later

Big Business

Companies that produced goods began to make a lot of money. Ordinary people wanted to get rich, too. They started buying stocks in companies. A stock is a part or share of a company that can be bought and sold.

Risky Business

Some people spent their entire life savings on stocks. Many people borrowed money to buy them. They planned to sell their shares for a profit and pay their **debts**. Stock prices had been steadily rising for years and no one expected them to fall.

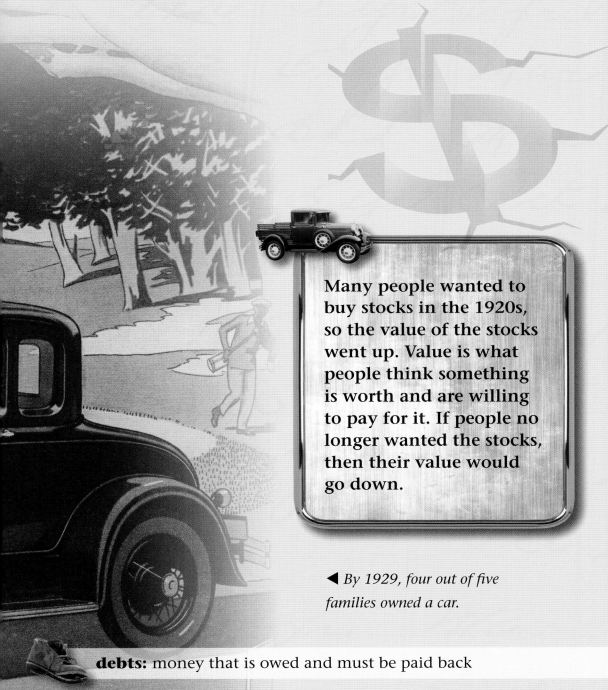

Many people wanted to buy stocks in the 1920s, so the value of the stocks went up. Value is what people think something is worth and are willing to pay for it. If people no longer wanted the stocks, then their value would go down.

◀ *By 1929, four out of five families owned a car.*

debts: money that is owed and must be paid back

Record High

On September 3, 1929, the value of stocks reached their highest point ever. **Investors** were thrilled! They had played the stock market and won! They would all be rich! It looked like the Roaring Twenties would keep roaring along right into the 1930s.

▲ *A stock exchange is a place where shares are bought and sold. People traded shares in New York (above), London, Toronto, Montreal, Tokyo, and other stock exchanges around the world.*

Bad News

Then worrisome news stories began to affect stock prices. People learned that a top British investor had been selling fake stocks. News also spread that the United States wanted to raise fees on goods coming into the country. It was all bad news for the stock market.

▶ *This picture shows stock market clerks studying falling prices on ticker tape on October 25, 1929. Stock ticker machines sent stock reports quickly around the world.*

"All the money I took in, I put into stocks. The first day of October in 1929 made me feel like I was rich ... I figured I could pay my debts any time, and I just let them ride."

George Mehales, a Greek immigrant who lost all his money in the stock market and was forced to sell his restaurant at rock-bottom prices

investors: people who buy goods in order to make a profit

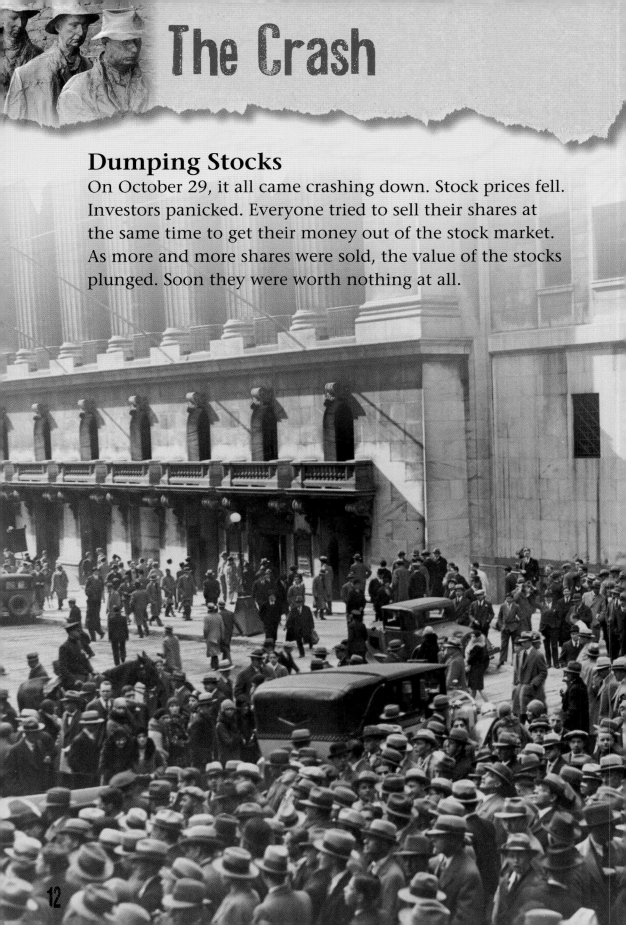

The Crash

Dumping Stocks

On October 29, it all came crashing down. Stock prices fell. Investors panicked. Everyone tried to sell their shares at the same time to get their money out of the stock market. As more and more shares were sold, the value of the stocks plunged. Soon they were worth nothing at all.

Losing Everything

Billions of dollars were lost that day. Many Americans were instantly broke. They were left with huge debts that they could not repay. Worried investors crowded city streets looking for answers. How would they pay their bills and feed their families?

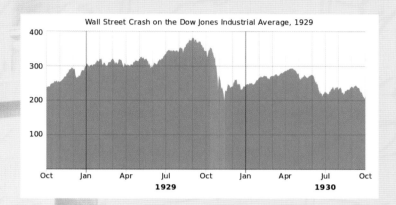

▲ *This chart shows the rise and then sudden fall of stock prices in 1929 and 1930.*

"It came with a speed and **ferocity** that left men dazed. The bottom simply fell out of the market... Where was it going to end?"

1929 report on the stock market crash in *The New York Times*

◄ *Crowds of people rushed to Wall Street after the crash. Wall Street is the area in New York where people buy and sell stocks.*

ferocity: fierceness

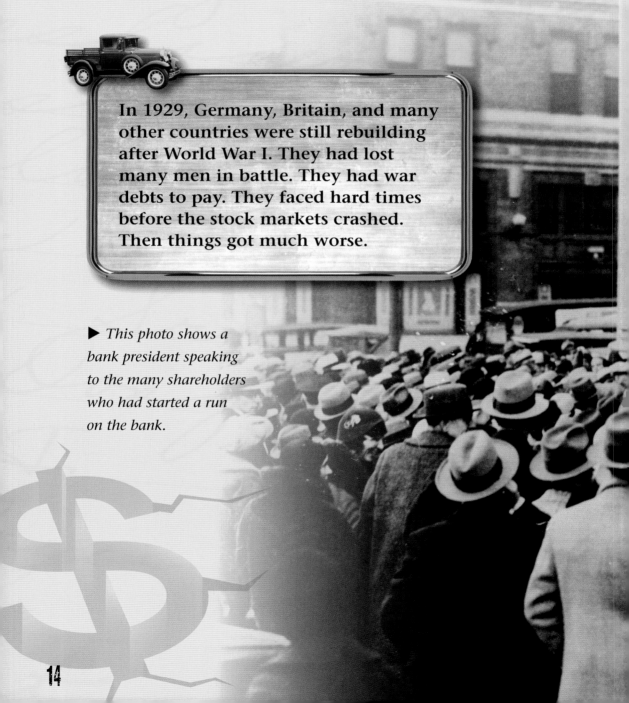

Worldwide Panic

News of the **disaster** spread quickly to other countries. The value of stocks everywhere dropped. Investors hurried to stock exchanges in Toronto, London, Sydney, and other cities around the world. People tried to sell their shares and cut their losses. Most were too late.

In 1929, Germany, Britain, and many other countries were still rebuilding after World War I. They had lost many men in battle. They had war debts to pay. They faced hard times before the stock markets crashed. Then things got much worse.

▶ *This photo shows a bank president speaking to the many shareholders who had started a run on the bank.*

Bank Runs

Some banks lost all their money when the markets crashed. They were forced to close their doors for good. People rushed to the banks that were still open to get their life savings. The banks soon ran out of money. People who came late lost everything.

disaster: a sudden event that causes great loss or hardship

Out of Business

Many companies lost money when the markets crashed and the banks closed. Some went out of business right away. They shut down their factories and turned their workers away. Other companies cut back the hours and pay of their workers to stay in business.

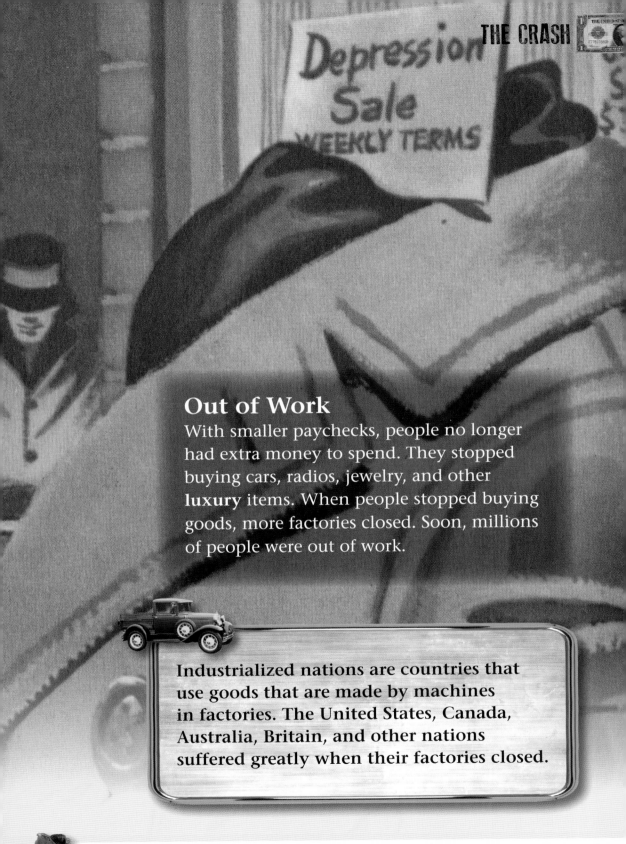

Out of Work

With smaller paychecks, people no longer had extra money to spend. They stopped buying cars, radios, jewelry, and other **luxury** items. When people stopped buying goods, more factories closed. Soon, millions of people were out of work.

Industrialized nations are countries that use goods that are made by machines in factories. The United States, Canada, Australia, Britain, and other nations suffered greatly when their factories closed.

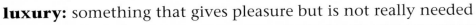

luxury: something that gives pleasure but is not really needed

STEADY JOB

NOT LAZ

WE DON'T WANT
SYMPATH
WE WANT
WORK

STOP US

We Want Work!

By 1932, one out of every four workers in the United States was **unemployed**. People were also out of work in Canada, Australia, and Germany. They were good, hard-working men who wanted to earn an honest living. But there were no jobs for them.

▼ *People tried everything to get jobs. These unemployed men put signs on their car begging for work.*

WE WANT A STEAD
YEAR AROUND JO
WITH REASONABLE
WAGE. NOT LAZY.
IF INTERESTED
STOP US

MAKE OFFER

AMB

> **"My dad was the strongest man I knew, but the Depression brought him to his knees."**
>
> Travis, a 12-year-old boy who found his unemployed father crying behind their house

Men's Work

In the 1930s, women did not usually have jobs outside the home. They cooked, cleaned, and cared for children. The family depended on the men of the household to pay the bills. During the Depression, men often felt deeply ashamed that they could not find work and take care of their families.

unemployed: jobless or out of work

Some Relief

Many families survived on **relief** from the government. In some countries, unemployed workers got a small supply of food each month. In other places, they got small sums of money. It was never enough to take good care of their families, however.

◀ *These unemployed men are queuing outside a soup kitchen in Chicago.*

Work Camps

In Canada, the government started relief camps for unmarried men who needed jobs. Thousands of men worked long, hard hours building and planting for just 20 cents a day. They lived in shacks and had little food to eat. The men were free to leave the work camps but had nowhere else to go.

"Food and jobs were hard to get and many people stood in lines for government hand-outs. A lot of people lived on powdered milk, dried beans, and potatoes."

Bill, a teenager during the Depression

relief: food, money, and other help given to those in need

Selling to Survive

People did whatever they could to survive during the Great Depression. Many people sold their cars, pianos, jewelry, and other prized belongings. People were **desperate** for cash and sold the items for much less than they were worth.

▶ *Many men rode the rails to find work. Few found what they were looking for.*

Many children were forced to quit school and get jobs to help pay their family's bills. They worked in factories, canneries, mines, and fields. Children also looked after their brothers and sisters so their mothers could get jobs.

Riding the Rails

Many men left their families in search of work. They hitchhiked or hopped on freight trains and rode the rails for free. Some men sent home money and came back as soon as they could. Others could not find work and were too ashamed to ever return home.

desperate: willing to do anything due to an extreme need

No Rain

Even farmers had trouble feeding their families in the 1930s. There was a **drought** in the flat, grassy prairies of Canada and the United States. Without rain, crops could not grow. When the crops failed, the soil dried up and turned to dust.

In 1930, the United States made a law that raised fees on imports. Imports are crops, lumber, wool, and all other goods that come into a country. Other countries soon raised their fees in return. The high cost of imports hurt farmers and slowed trading around the world.

▼ *The 1930s were called the "Dirty Thirties." Thick dust covered houses and drifted through doors and windows. It landed on furniture and clothes and made everything dirty.*

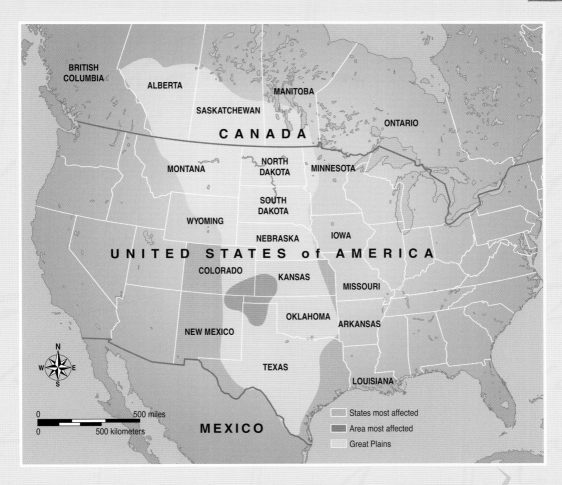

▲ *This map shows how the Southern Great Plains were most affected by the Dust Bowl.*

The Dust Bowl

High winds picked up the dust and carried it far away. Huge clouds of dust swirled over farms and towns. The dust destroyed crops and homes. It choked people and animals. This deadly period of time became known as the Dust Bowl.

drought: a long period of time with little or no rain

Nothing to Lose

Without crops to sell, farmers could not pay their bills. They lost their homes and their farms. Many families decided to try their luck elsewhere. They packed up their belongings and hit the open road.

On the Move

Hundreds of thousands of families left the prairies and moved west to find work. Some **migrants** made a little money picking fruit and other crops. The work lasted only for a short time, however. The migrants lived in tents and moved from farm to farm.

◀ *These farmers were moving from Texas to Arkansas hoping to harvest cotton. When the picture was taken, they had no money, no food, and only three gallons of gas for their truck.*

"I worked in hospitals. I tended bar. I cooked. I worked in the fields. I done a little bit of everything to make a living for my kids."

Florence Owens Thompson, remembering her life as a migrant worker

▲ *Men, women, (and children) worked long, hard days.*

migrants: people who move from place to place to find work

The Homeless

Many families lost their homes during the Great Depression. They could not afford to pay their rent or other bills. Homeless people were forced to move in with relatives or live on the streets. They huddled in doorways and slept on hard park benches.

Some lucky families were able to keep their homes. They made money by renting rooms to **boarders**. Many people lived together in dirty, crowded houses and apartments. Most homes did not have heat, electricity, running water, or indoor toilets.

▲ *This homeless family walked from Phoenix, Arizona, to San Diego, California, where they hoped to get relief.*

Shanty Towns

Some poor people found shelter in shanties, or shacks. They made the shanties out of tin, wood, cardboard, cloth, or other materials they found. Many people built shanties in parks or outside big cities. Over time, groups of shacks grew into large shanty towns.

boarders: people who pay to live in other people's homes

Mouths to Feed

Mothers struggled to feed their children. They made bread and simple meals such as soups and stews. They cooked with flour, potatoes, rice—and even weeds! Most families could not afford to buy milk, meat, fruits, or other foods they needed to stay healthy.

Breadlines

Men stood for hours in long breadlines. A breadline is a place where churches or **charities** hand out free soup, bread, and other foods. Children trapped birds, squirrels, and rabbits to eat. Families grew gardens. Everyone pitched in to put meals on the table.

"We haven't had anything in the house to eat for a week now but two messes of flour and a peck of meal. The children ... come home after school begging for food."

Mrs. Garrett, mother of six during the Great Depression

◄ *This picture shows a soup kitchen in New York City in 1931.*

charities: groups that help people in need

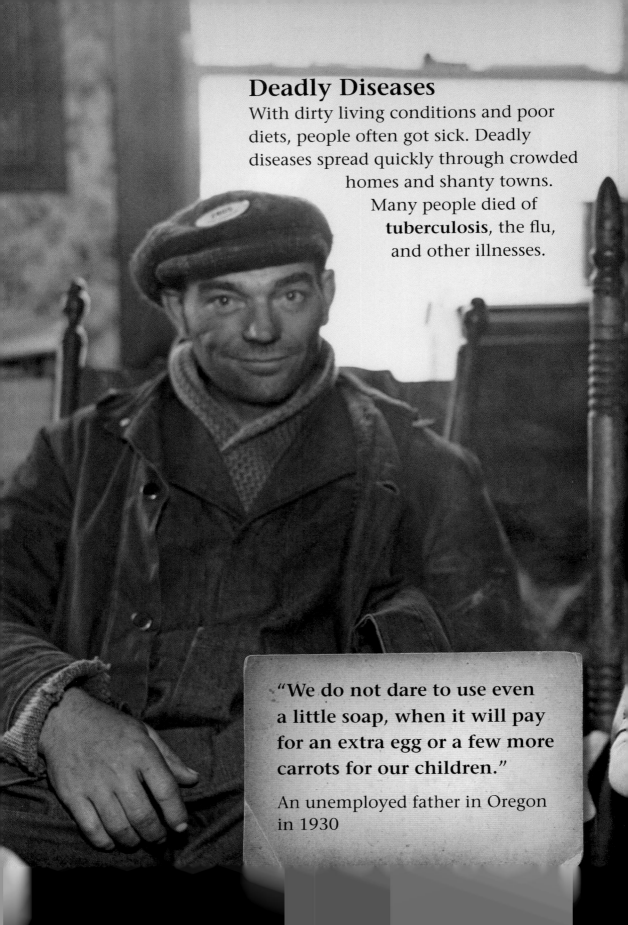

Deadly Diseases

With dirty living conditions and poor diets, people often got sick. Deadly diseases spread quickly through crowded homes and shanty towns. Many people died of **tuberculosis**, the flu, and other illnesses.

"We do not dare to use even a little soap, when it will pay for an extra egg or a few more carrots for our children."

An unemployed father in Oregon in 1930

No Doctors

When people got sick, they could not afford to pay for doctors or go to hospitals. They could not buy medicines to treat their diseases. Sick people prayed for good health and hoped for a miracle.

◀ *This poor family had tuberculosis and no money to treat it.*

▲ *Posters like this warned people about how the deadly disea_ was spread.*

tuberculosis: a lung disease that is spread through the air

Getting By

Even in the darkest days of the Depression, people found ways to get by and have fun. They played cards and baseball. They strummed guitars and sang about their troubles. They played the game of Monopoly and enjoyed getting rich— even if it was not real money.

▼ *This is the book cover for* Bound for Glory *by folk singer Woody Guthrie. The book tells of his life on the road during the Depression years.*

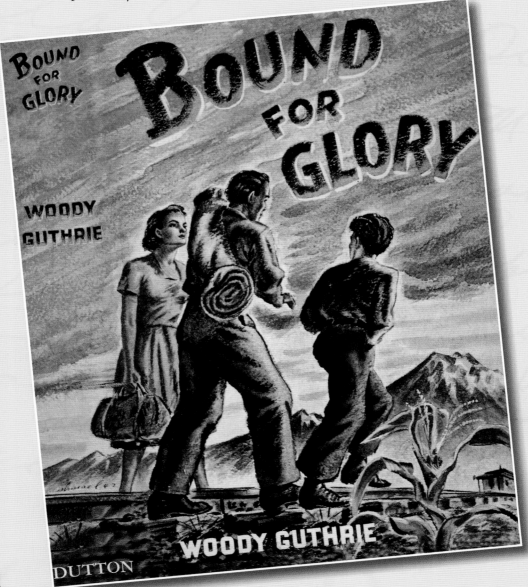

◀ *Shirley Temple was a child star whose movies were popular during the Depression. Her sunny musicals cheered the nation.*

Getting Away

People sometimes scraped up enough cash to go to the movies. They watched the moving pictures and forgot their cares for a while. Comedies, musicals, and crime films were popular. Fans gazed at the stars on the screen and dreamed of their riches.

Gangsters became **folk heroes**. Stories of shootouts with Bonnie and Clyde, John Dillinger, Pretty Boy Floyd, and other outlaws filled the news. These violent criminals robbed banks and stores, gave stolen money to the poor, killed police, and escaped the law for years.

folk heroes: ordinary people who fight against those in power

Herbert Hoover

Herbert Hoover was President of the United States from 1929 to 1933. During that time, things went from bad to worse. As the Depression wore on, people got hungrier— and angrier— with Hoover's government.

▶ *Hoover believed Americans should not depend on the government for help. He wanted people to support themselves. He also did not want the government to go into debt.*

Americans blamed President Hoover for their **poverty**. They called the shanty towns where poor people lived "Hoovervilles." Cars that had run out of gas and were pulled by horses were known as "Hoover wagons."

Not Enough

Hoover started programs to get the country working and building again. He led construction of the massive Hoover Dam and increased spending for other public works projects. He lent billions of dollars to banks, railroads, and companies to keep them in business. But it was too little, too late. Americans demanded change.

▲ *Thousands of workers were involved in building the Hoover Dam.*

poverty: a state of being very poor

The New President

In 1933, Franklin D. Roosevelt was elected President of the United States. Roosevelt promised to make changes that would improve the **economy**. His plan for the country was called the New Deal.

> "The skies above are clear again
> So let's sing a song of cheer again
> Happy days are here again."
>
> Lyrics from Roosevelt's campaign song, "Happy Days Are Here Again"

The New Deal

The New Deal gave food and emergency housing to the needy. It created millions of new jobs and set rules for fair wages. It gave money to unemployed workers, senior citizens, and people with disabilities. And it gave people new hope for the future.

◄ *Roosevelt's New Deal helped end the Depression and made Roosevelt a hero.*

economy: the money and resources in a country

Back to Business

The New Deal helped America get back to business. But the biggest boost to the economy was World War II. The war began in Europe on September 1, 1939. Soon countries around the world were busy fighting or helping the war effort with food and manufacturing.

▶ *Working women kept factories in business while men were away at war.*

Ready for War

American companies built weapons, ships, and planes for the **Allies**. Women worked in factories. Men grew food or trained to be soldiers. The United States entered World War II on December 8, 1941. The Great Depression had ended and the world was ready to fight a new battle.

Canadian Prime Minister R.B. Bennett followed Roosevelt's lead and made a New Deal for Canada. Bennett introduced fair wages and hours for workers. He paid money to unemployed workers, farmers, and seniors. The New Deal helped Canada but could not save Bennett's career. He lost the 1935 election to Mackenzie King.

Allies: countries including Britain, France, the U.S., and Canad

The Economy Today

Ups and Downs

The Great Depression ended more than 70 years ago. Since then, the world's economies have had many ups and downs. The changes are part of a pattern called the business cycle. A pattern is something that repeats over time.

The Business Cycle

There are periods when businesses grow and there are plenty of jobs. The economy is good—but it is too good to last. Then business slows, people lose their jobs, and times get tough. When the economy slows, it is called a **recession**. When things are very bad for a long period, it is called a depression. Over time, the economy starts to improve again.

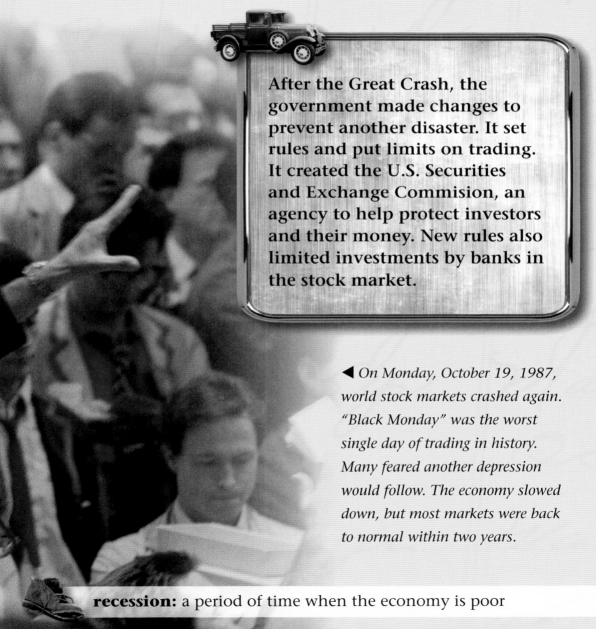

After the Great Crash, the government made changes to prevent another disaster. It set rules and put limits on trading. It created the U.S. Securities and Exchange Commision, an agency to help protect investors and their money. New rules also limited investments by banks in the stock market.

◀ On Monday, October 19, 1987, world stock markets crashed again. "Black Monday" was the worst single day of trading in history. Many feared another depression would follow. The economy slowed down, but most markets were back to normal within two years.

recession: a period of time when the economy is poor

The Great Recession

In 2007, a major worldwide recession began. The value of stocks and houses plunged. People owed more money on their homes than they were worth. Companies went out of business and banks almost went **bankrupt**. There was danger of another depression.

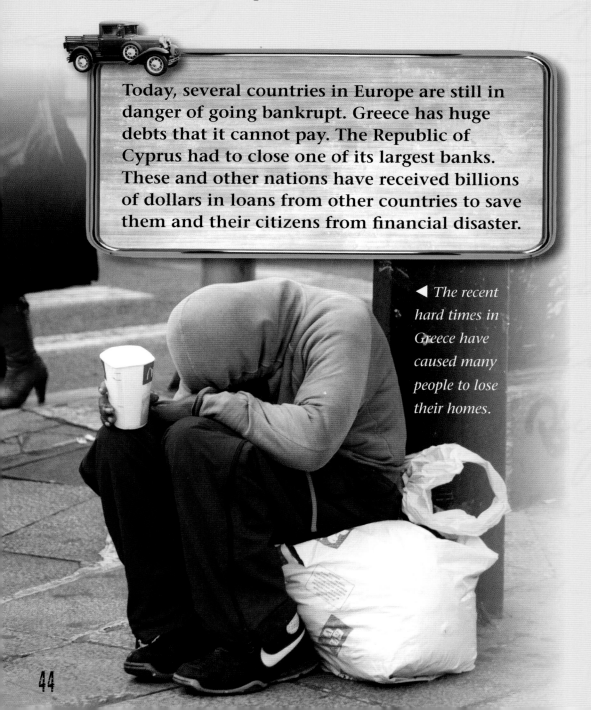

Today, several countries in Europe are still in danger of going bankrupt. Greece has huge debts that it cannot pay. The Republic of Cyprus had to close one of its largest banks. These and other nations have received billions of dollars in loans from other countries to save them and their citizens from financial disaster.

◀ *The recent hard times in Greece have caused many people to lose their homes.*

Big Bailouts

This time, governments around the world stepped in to help before it was too late. They bought stocks and lent billions of dollars to banks to protect people's savings. They gave huge loans to car companies that were going bankrupt to keep people employed. The world economy was saved from collapse but not every country has fully recovered.

▲ *Traders celebrate a good day at the New York Stock Exchange and what they hope is a step on the road to economic recovery.*

 bankrupt: being out of money and unable to pay back debts

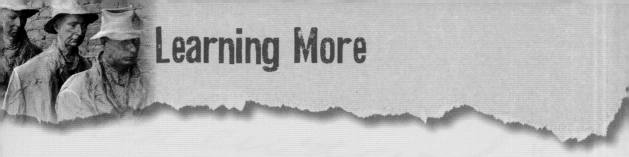

Books

Cornerstones of Freedom: The Great Depression
by Melissa McDaniel
(Scholastic, 2012)

Not a Nickel to Spare: The Great Depression Diary of Sally Cohen
by Perry Nodelman
(Scholastic Canada Ltd., 2007)

The Great Depression: A Migrant Mother's Story
by Dorothy Alexander Sugarman
(Teacher Created Materials, 2009)

The Great Depression: A Primary Source History (In Their Own Words)
by Stanley Schultz
(Gareth Stevens Publishing, 2005)

The Great Depression: An Interactive History Adventure
by Michael Burgan
(Capstone Press, 2011)

Movies

American Experience: Riding the Rails
A non-fiction PBS film produced in 2003

American Experience: Surviving the Dust Bowl
A non-fiction film made by PBS in 2007

Websites

http://americanhistory.pppst.com/greatdepression.html
American History: The Great Depression

http://www.digitalhistory.uh.edu/learning_history/children_depression/depression_children_menu.cfm
Digital History Explorations: Children and the Great Depression

Glossary

Allies Countries including Britain, France, the U.S., and Canada

bankrupt Being out of money and unable to pay back debts

boarders People who pay to live in other people's homes

charities Groups that help people in need

credit A way of buying goods but paying for them later

debts Money that is owed and must be paid back

desperate Willing to do anything due to an extreme need

disaster A sudden event that causes great loss or hardship

drought A long period of time with little or no rain

economy The money and resources in a country

ferocity Fierceness

folk heroes Ordinary people who fight against those in power

investors People who buy goods in order to make a profit

luxury Something that gives pleasure but is not really needed

migrants People who move from place to place to find work

poverty A state of being very poor

recession A period of time when the economy is poor

relief Food, money, and other help given to those in need

stock market A place where stocks are bought and sold

tuberculosis A lung disease that is spread through the air

unemployed Jobless or out of work

Index

Entries in **bold** refer to pictures